BROKEN BONES

ELAINE LANDAU

Marshall Cavendish
Benchmark
New York

Marshall Cavendish Benchmark
99 White Plains Road
Tarrytown, New York 10591
www.marshallcavendish.us

Expert Reader: Leslie L. Barton, M.D., professor of Pediatrics, University of Arizona College of Medicine, Tucson, Arizona

Library of Congress Cataloging-in-Publication Data
Landau, Elaine.
  Broken bones / Elaine Landau.
       p. cm. — (Head-to-toe health)
  Summary: "Provides basic information about the skeletal system, broken bones, and prevention"—Provided by publisher.
  Includes bibliographical references and index.
  ISBN 978-0-7614-2847-3
  1. Fractures—Juvenile literature. 2. Bones—Juvenile literature. I. Title. II. Series.
RD101.L337 2009
617.1 5—dc22
2007026665

Editor: Christine Florie
Publisher: Michelle Bisson
Art Director: Anahid Hamparian
Series Designer: Alex Ferrari

Photo research by Connie Gardner

Cover photo by Pixtail/RF/Art Life Images

The photographs in this book are used with permission and through the courtesy of:
Corbis: John-Francis Bourke/zefa, 4; Bob Winsett, 7; Jose Luis Palez, 21; The Image Works: Bill Bachman, 17; Jeff Greenberg, 23; Peter H. Vizdak, 24; SuperStock: Robert Huberman, 6; age fotostock , 15; Getty Images: Stone, 8; David Deas, 12; PhotoResearchers: Michel Gilles, 9; Salisbury District Hospital, 11; PhotoEdit: Myrleen Ferguson, 19.

Printed in China
1 3 5 6 4 2

CONTENTS

ALL ABOUT YOUR BONES

Have you ever seen a skyscraper being built? Beneath its walls is a steel framework. It's sometimes called a skeleton framework. The framework holds up the building and gives it its form.

You can't see the skeleton framework in the finished building. Yet you know it's there. It is doing its job in supporting the skyscraper.

YOU'VE GOT SOMETHING IN COMMON WITH A SKYSCRAPER

In some ways, your body is like a tall building. You have a skeleton, too. You see lots of skeletons every Halloween on greeting cards and posters. But there's a real one beneath your skin. It's made up of bones.

◀ There are no "bones" about it, keeping healthy and fit builds strong bones and helps prevent breaks.

The dried out bones of a Halloween skeleton look dead. Yet the bones in your body are very much alive. Your bones are made of living **cells**. As you grow, your bones grow with you. They don't stop growing until you've reached your full adult size.

YOU NEED YOUR BONES

Your bones are light, but strong. They support the weight of your body. You wouldn't look the way you do if you didn't have bones. Think about all the boneless creatures in nature. Can you imagine having a body like a jellyfish, slug, or clam?

Your bones, along with your muscles, also allow you to do many things. The muscles and bones in your leg and foot let you kick a soccer ball.

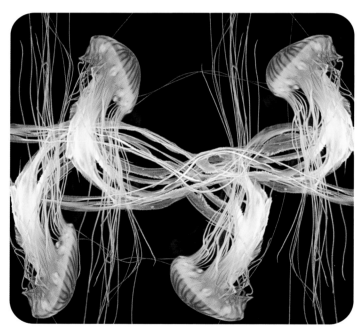

Jellyfish have soft bodies because they have no bones. They are made up of 95 percent water.

The strong bones and muscles in this girl's legs help support her body while she ice skates.

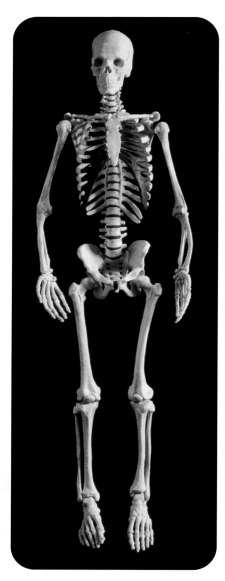

Those in your hand let you write a letter and play computer games.

Your bones are really useful in other ways, too. They protect your body's important **organs**. Your rib cage is made up of a set of twenty-four curved bones in your chest. It protects your heart and lungs.

Every adult has 206 bones. You are actually born with even more bones. However, some **fuse** or grow together as you grow up.

Some of your bones are large, while others are small. Bones come in different shapes as well. Yet each is important. You need strong, healthy bones for a full, active life.

The 206 bones in the human body are living forms, each with a job to do.

Your bones are made up of various layers. The hardest part of the bone is called **compact bone**. Beneath it is a layer known as **spongy bone**. It's called that because it looks a little like a sponge.

Spongy bone produces red **bone marrow**. Red bone marrow creates both red and white blood cells. The red cells carry oxygen to different parts of your body. White blood cells are important, too. They help fight disease and infection.

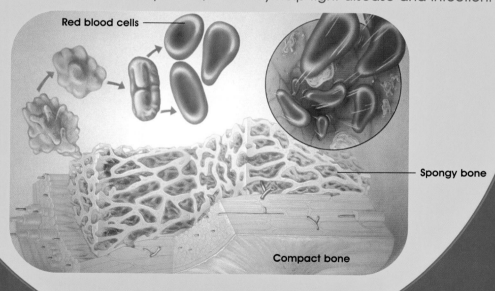

Red blood cells

Spongy bone

Compact bone

When Your Bones Break

It's the first snowfall of winter. You're going skiing with your dad and brother. They ski down the slope first.

Now it's your turn. You're going down the slope at a good speed. Then suddenly you lose your balance. You feel your legs buckle beneath you and you fall.

BAM! Much of your weight lands on your leg. You hear a snapping sound, and when you try to move your leg, it really hurts.

Other skiers come to help you. Your father is among them. "Don't try to get up," he says. "Your leg may be broken."

BREAKING A BONE

Broken bones are not uncommon among active young people. A break in a bone is called a fracture. There are different types of fractures, or breaks. A few of these are described here.

A **hairline fracture** is a slim or very narrow crack in a bone. It is a less serious break than some of the other types of fractures. However, a hairline fracture can still be quite painful.

You may have heard the terms **open fracture** and **comminuted fracture**. Here the breaks are worse. With an open fracture, a piece of the bone has come through the skin. Open fractures are sometimes also called compound fractures.

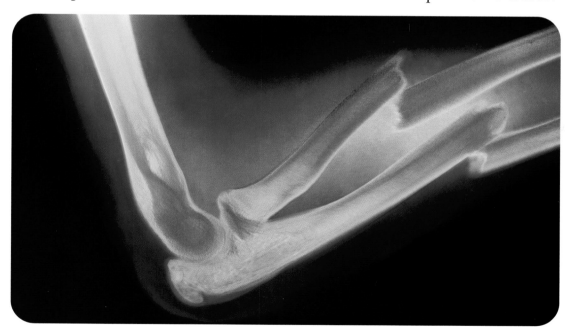

A colored X-ray shows a compound fracture. The sharp broken ends of each bone can break through the skin.

In a comminuted fracture, the bone has been broken into a number of pieces. In these cases, the bone may also be crushed.

Children's bones are able to bend more than adults', but with enough pressure will snap and break.

BONES BEND ... A LITTLE

Your bones are hard—yet they will bend a bit. Imagine bending a plastic ruler. It can bend a little. When you stop, the ruler springs back to its original shape. But if you bend it too far, the ruler will break.

Your bones act the same way. They will bend slightly. However, if too much force is applied to them, they will snap or break. You're left with a broken bone.

IT'S GREAT TO BE A KID

Nevertheless, there's some good news, too. Children's bones bend more easily than adults'. They are also less likely to break. When a child's bone does break, it usually heals more quickly than an adult's. So if you're a kid, you're in luck when it comes to bones.

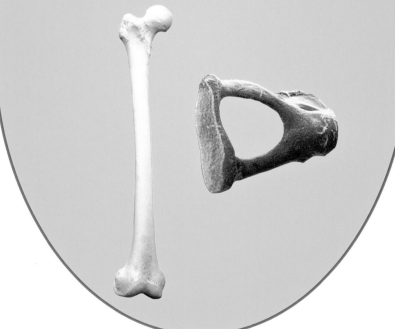

Did you know that the largest bone in your body is the femur? (below left). That's your thighbone. The smallest bone in your body is the stirrup (below right). The stirrup is a tiny bone behind your eardrum. It's less than a fraction of an inch long.

You Were with Your Friend When . . .

Oh, no! You were skateboarding with your friend and he fell. It looks like he's hurt. He can't get up. What should you do?

DON'T PANIC

Don't force your friend to get up. You should not move the injured person in any way. If you think a bone could be broken, neither you nor your friend should try to straighten the bone. Even if the bone has broken through the skin, do not push it back down. Moving a broken bone this way can sometimes cause damage to blood vessels, nerves, and other tissues.

In some accidents, there may be more than one broken bone. It may be necessary to call an ambulance. Do not try to handle this all on your own. Quickly find a responsible adult to help you and your friend.

Accidents do happen. Be sure to get help from an adult.

SIGNS OF A BROKEN BONE

There are some common signs or symptoms of a broken bone. If a bone is broken, the area around it will be painful. There will soon be swelling as well. The injured person will have trouble using that bone and there may be bruising or redness.

Sometimes a doctor can tell if a bone is broken just by looking at it. Other times, the doctor will need to feel the possible break. In any case, the doctor needs to know as much as possible about the fracture.

Therefore, an **X-ray** needs to be taken. When taking an X-ray, a machine is used to produce a special picture. This picture allows the doctor to see a part of your body beneath your skin. With an X-ray, the doctor can usually tell the type of fracture you have and what needs to be done.

DID YOU KNOW?

Broken bones are the fourth most common injury among children younger than age six. Children tend to have more broken bones in the spring and summer. That may be partly because of the warm weather. Young people are more likely to be outdoors, running, jumping, and taking part in different sports.

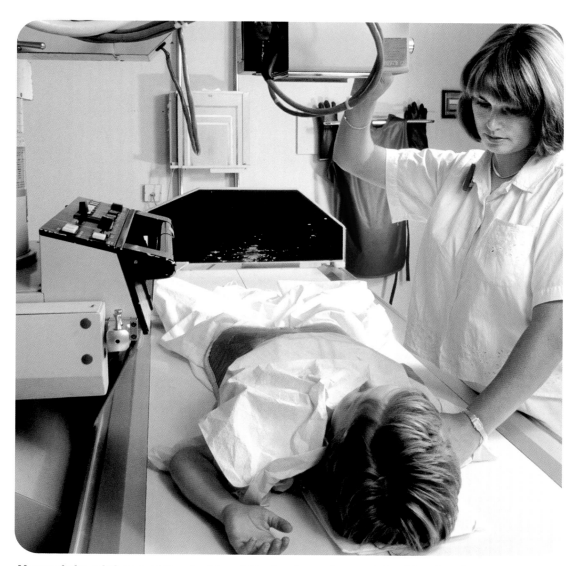

X-rays take pictures of the inside of the body and can detect broken bones.

TREATMENT–
BROKEN BONES HEAL

It is important to get medical care for a broken bone. A doctor will **realign,** or set the bone. In doing this, the doctor usually pulls or pushes the bone back into place. Sometimes, a break is more serious. Then the doctor may have to operate to properly place the bone.

A broken bone should not be moved until it is healed. There's a reason for this. As the bone heals, its ends "knit" together. New bone develops around the break so that the pieces join together. This cannot happen if the bone is moved about.

GETTING A CAST

How can you keep a broken bone from moving? Most doctors will put it in a sling or cast. This keeps the bone in its proper position while it heals. It also eases the pain.

A cast is sort of like a special bandage. Many casts are made of plaster. This plaster comes from a heavy white powder called plaster of paris. When water is added to plaster of paris, it forms a thick paste. This hardens to become a cast.

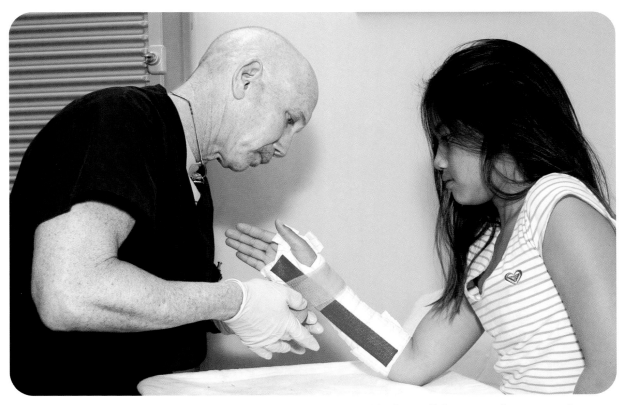

After a broken bone is put back in place, a cast is used to keep it from moving around while it heals.

Plaster of paris is often used in school art projects. You may have used it to make things in the past. But if you break a bone, it's likely that you'll be wearing it instead.

Other casts are made of fiberglass. Fiberglass is a type of plastic. Fiberglass casts tend to be lighter and stronger than plaster casts. Plaster casts are white, while fiberglass casts come in different colors.

LIVING WITH A CAST

Plaster casts are not waterproof. So it's important to keep them dry. Some people cover their casts with a plastic bag when they shower or take a bath. Others just use a wet sponge to stay clean.

Be sure to tell the person taking care of you if your cast starts to crack. This can happen if it's hit or if the cast has a weak spot. Also, tell that person right away if your fingers or toes begin to turn

HERE'S A COOL TIP

As you begin to heal, the skin beneath your cast may feel itchy. Don't stick anything inside your cast to scratch it. You can do more damage than good that way.

Instead, set your hairdryer on the coolest setting possible. Then blow the cool air into your cast. This often brings some relief.

white or bluish, or feel numb, tingle, or hurt while you're wearing your cast.

BE CREATIVE!

Wearing a cast may not be fun, but sometimes it's necessary. Try to make the best of it. Lots of people like to have their casts decorated by family and friends.

Some casts are decorated with permanent markers. Others with stickers. It's also always fun to have your friends sign your cast.

Remember that you won't be wearing your cast forever. Soon it will be off. Before you know it your broken bone will be healed.

Some like to have their cast decorated by family and friends.

PREVENTING BROKEN BONES

Do you enjoy sports and playing outdoors? Being active doesn't mean that sooner or later you'll break a bone. Often, you can help keep your bones strong and healthy. Many people never break a bone.

TAKE A TIP FROM POPEYE

Remember Popeye the Sailor? He ate spinach for extra strength. Spinach contains calcium, and that helps build strong bones. Follow Popeye's lead and eat your spinach!

EAT THE RIGHT WAY EVERYDAY

A well-balanced diet is important in keeping your bones strong. Your diet should include foods that contain the mineral **calcium**. Your body needs calcium for strong bones and teeth.

Ice cream is a delicious way to get bone-building calcium.

You can get calcium from a glass of milk or calcium fortified orange juice, a grilled cheese sandwich, or a serving of macaroni and cheese. There's also calcium in broccoli, kale, collard greens, dry roasted almonds, and sesame seeds. Pudding made with milk has calcium, and so does cheese pizza, string cheese, yogurt, and even ice cream!

GET MOVING

Exercise is also important in building strong bones. However, not just any type of exercise will do. For your bones to benefit, you need to do weight-bearing exercise.

A weight-bearing activity is any sport or exercise that puts some stress on your bones. Your bone cells react to this stress by making your bones stronger. Weight-bearing activities include walking, hiking, basketball, soccer, dancing, jogging, tennis, and volleyball.

Being active is a great way to strengthen your bones.

Karate, tae kwon do, jumping rope, and stair-climbing are also weight-bearing activities. For good bone health, you need to do between thirty-five and sixty minutes of weight-bearing activity daily.

Swimming, bike riding, and skateboarding will help you keep fit. But they will not strengthen your bones. That's because when you swim, the water actually bears your weight. Therefore, your bones don't get the benefit of the activity. The same thing happens when you're on a bike or skateboard. It's a good idea to mix up your activities. Just be sure to include some weight-bearing ones!

HEALTH ALERT

In recent years there's been an increase in forearm breaks in young people. The forearm is the part of your arm between your elbow and wrist. Some researchers think that these breaks may be due to a decrease in bone mass in children. This could be the result of more young people drinking soda instead of milk. It may also be more common among kids who watch television and play video games instead of exercise.

HAVE FUN, BUT BE CAREFUL

It's great to be active, but young people often break bones when playing hard or climbing. So think about where you do these things. Sometimes, there's a choice of where to play.

If possible, pass on playgrounds with hard concrete surfaces. Is there a place nearby where there are soft mats or wood chips? That would be a better choice.

Have fun, but be smart. Don't be tempted to try dangerous stunts at the playground. The same goes for stunts on bikes and skateboards and where cars are nearby. There are better ways to impress your friends.

Only use playground equipment the way it's supposed to be used. Remember that a broken bone can keep you on the sidelines for weeks. That's no fun.

Do you play sports? Wearing kneepads during games can help protect your bones. The same goes for wrist pads. Protect your bones when you go biking, too. Be sure to wear your helmet.

Your bones are important to your health. You'll need them for the rest of your life. Proper diet and exercise will help you keep your bones strong. Just add a little extra care when you play. That's a winning recipe for avoiding broken bones.

GLOSSARY

bone marrow — soft, fatty tissue that fills the inside of most bones

calcium — a mineral needed for strong healthy bones

comminuted fracture — a fracture in which the bone is crushed or has been broken into a number of pieces

compact bone — the hard layer of bone

cells — the basic units of all living things

fuse — to join together

hairline fracture — a thin or very narrow crack in a bone

organs — parts of the body that do particular jobs

open fracture — a broken bone in which a piece of the bone has come through the skin

realign — to set a bone or put it back into its proper position

spongy bone — the inner layer of bone that creates bone marrow

X-ray — a special type of picture that allows a doctor to see beneath your skin

FIND OUT MORE

BOOKS

Ganeri, Anita. *Your Muscles and Bones*. Milwaukee, WI: Gareth Stevens Publications, 2003.

Gold, Susan Dudley. *The Musculoskeletal System and the Skin*. Berkeley Heights, NJ: Enslow Publishers, 2003.

Houghton, Gillian. *Bones: The Skeletal System*. New York: PowerKids, 2007.

Olien, Rebecca. *The Skeletal System*. Mankato, MN: Capstone, 2006.

Royston, Angela. *Broken Bones*. Chicago: Heinemann, 2004.

Ziefert, Harriet. *You Can't See Your Bones with Binoculars: A Guide to Your 206 Bones*. Maplewood, NJ: Blue Apple Books, 2003.

WEB SITES

Bonezone

www.bonezone.org.uk/

Visit this fun Web site on bones. Don't miss the "fun for kids" link. There are lots of bone puzzles and games here.

Got Milk?

www.got-milk.com/

Check out this great Web site on why milk is important for strong bones. You'll find lots of games, cow jokes, and fun recipes for kids.

INDEX

Page numbers in **boldface** are illustrations

ABOUT THE AUTHOR

Award-winning author Elaine Landau has written over three hundred books for young readers. Many of these are on health and science topics.

Ms. Landau received her bachelor's degree in English and Journalism from New York University and a master's degree in Library and Information Science from Pratt Institute. You can visit Elaine Landau at her Web site: www.elainelandau.com.